The International Design Library

ANCIENT SCANDINAVIAN DESIGNS

Bev Ulsrud Van Berkom

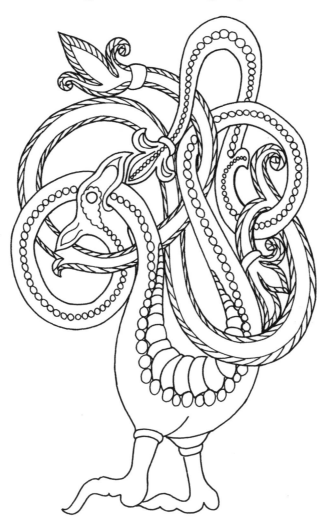

Stemmer House
PUBLISHERS, INC.

Owings Mills, Maryland

Introduction

THE ANCIENT SCANDINAVIANS were a fiercely independent people who lived entirely by their own rules. Their art mirrored the restless, mysterious people themselves and so it helps to know something about them. The art spans a period beginning with the Migration Period, when all of Europe went seeking, trading and warring—none more aggressively than the Vikings—to the time when Christianity had finally established a firm toehold in the Northern lands.

That period came to be known as the Viking Age. For a few hundred years around 700 AD these Northern people catapulted into world view, and after 1200 AD were absorbed into Roman ways as Christianity took over. During that 500-year span England, Ireland, France and the other European countries felt the thrust of Viking restlessness, and were never to be the same again.

The origin of the word "viking" is unclear. It may have come from the word "vika" meaning creek — especially those leading out to sea. The early Scandinavians did not refer to themselves as Vikings, but the word has come to be inextricably associated with the people, referring specifically to the land-lacking second sons and others who went raiding and seeking their fortunes in the rest of the world.

Of the total early Scandinavian population, these represented only a small part. The majority of people in what later became known as Norway, Sweden and Denmark stayed home and lived relatively peaceful lives. There was no real national state during this time, just as there was no centralized society in the early years. People lived in small pockets and developed independently until the early fifth century AD. Late in the Viking Age more specific classifications developed.

"Karls" made up the largest class. This middle group was free; could own land; and had the right to bear arms. A much smaller class was called "Jarls" and was made up of kings, earls and the greatest of the chieftains. The third class was called "Thralls" and was the lowest. Little better than slaves, they had no legal rights, could not carry arms and were bound to their masters from birth.

Women were treated with the same respect as men. The women ruled the homes, carrying on their belts the keys, which became their badge of authority and honor. They could hold land in their own name and were often left in full charge of the land and family as their men went sailing.

Values of the early Scandinavians were practical and honor-loving: the *Havamal* (Sayings of the High One) gives directions to treat guests well, to provide a warm fire, water and towels. It tells that the best thing to carry in travels is a keen and sensible mind; for fools are detected anywhere. One is instructed not to boast of one's wisdom; to watch the beer one drinks if one would stay master of his mind. It explains that to understand how other people think, it is necessary to travel a great deal in the world; to stay faithful to one's friends, and above all, to be honest.

As the Northmen traveled in the world, their culture was deeply affected, too, by the customs of the places they visited. The Vikings were quick to absorb what interested them from other cultures. This included practical items like buttons and weapons as well as the ornamental motifs and decorations of the foreign art. From about the fifth century AD on, the Roman Empire made its influence felt in Europe. Although the northern countries of Scandinavia were not brought under Roman rule, they did take on some of their ways of life.

Trade ranged from Rome to Russia, the Byzantine Empire and the Scandinavian countries. Possession of rich exports became marks of prestige by Viking chieftains and wealthy farmers. Northern furs and leathers were traded for gold and silver, melted down and formed into jewelry worn by both men and women.

The Nordic people loved embellishment. Rich carvings were done on their boats, their house doorposts; they named and decorated their weapons, their jewelry, their horse's trappings. Their favorite motifs were fantastic bird and animal forms. Since these forms resemble nothing we are familiar with, their origins must remain part of the mysterious, lost traditions of ancient Scandinavia.

Vines and tendrils, popular elsewhere in Europe during this time, failed to interest the Vikings, and not until the late middle period did foliate designs appear with any regularity.

The embellishment or ornamentation was not meant to be just surface decoration. The Scandinavians believed that the fabulous animal and bird forms lent their spirits to the objects on which their images rested. No wonder the fierce animal heads on the ship's prows were taken down before approaching land. Otherwise the land spirits would be frightened off!

Images of the ships themselves were popular motifs on stone monuments. The tradition of stone monuments or "picture-stones" was already old on the island of Gotland at the beginning of the Viking Age. These stones were upright cylinder- or mushroom-shaped rocks, incised with pictures depicting myth scenes and figures or other motifs. Some of the earliest stones can be traced back to the classical world, with motifs such as the Greek wave patterns and meanders. Horse-baiting was a popular sport throughout Scandinavia, and is shown on a few picture-stones. Other stone monuments picture large wheel-decorations, sometimes with two smaller circles, symbolizing the sun or moon.

"Picture-stones" also contain short messages or memorial passages in the form of rune writing. Runes or the futhark were believed to have been given to the Viking god Odin after he hung nine nights and days without water or food on the "windy tree," probably referring to the great ash tree, Yggdrasil. Runes also were used as carriers of magical charms. One of the myths tells how Allfather Odin cut magic runes in the teeth of his eight-legged horse, Sleipnir, for protection in battle.

No other written records were left by the ancient Scandinavians. Theirs was an oral tradition. The written information we do have about the Vikings comes from twelfth-century manuscripts written by Icelander Snorri Sturluson and work written by priests and monks. Some bias might be expected to exist in the latter work, since these were the people warred against by the Vikings.

Artifacts provide the other major sources of information. Too few of these have come to light since much of their work was done on wood and these have deteriorated and disappeared over the centuries. Most of the art of the early Scandinavians has been lost for the same reason.

Jewelry and metal coins turn up at times as hoards are uncovered from the earth — mute testimony to the fact that their owners were not able to come back to claim them. Roman coins and medals were of great interest to the Vikings, and they adapted them to their own taste. Intrigued with the imagery of the emperor found on Roman coins and medals, the Viking artists quickly loosened the style, making it more abstract and symbolic.

The resulting circular objects were called bracteates; they were fitted with a channel so that they could be suspended from the neck or waist and worn as amulets. About half of the many bracteates found show a large human head resting on what appears to be a horse. Horses had religious significance and were symbols of fertility. Some bracteates show a highly stylized horse alone, and on some, mystical symbols, stars and dots appear.

As time went on the forms became more and more distorted until only the experienced eye could trace the intriguing chaos that resulted. This suited the artists and the general population of these northern countries.

There is evidence that the early Scandinavians were perfectly capable of rendering natural, representational forms. Realistic images of horses or people have been found scratched on the backs of jewelry or other artifacts. A very few early works did contain figures of natural-looking horses and other animals, but these forms do not seem to have become a tradition.

Ship graves have unearthed the most important artifact finds. The custom of ship burials was practiced by kings, chieftains and wealthy men and women from the fifth century AD onward. The belief that one could travel to the after-world by boat was very popular. These ships were outfitted with all the needs of Viking life and are excellent clues to how they lived. Kitchen utensils, weaving tools, jewelry, wagons and sledges were all provided. Coins were not often found, indicating they may have been family wealth. Horses, oxen and other animals were killed and added to the ship-grave.

Wall-hangings, rich clothing, food such as apples, nuts, grains, herbs and spices and vegetables have all been found in abundance. Horns of cattle were carved in an ornamental fashion and fitted with metal mounts. These were used for beer and mead, making the last voyage of more comfort to the dead occupant. Loaded with all these goods, the ships were pushed away from shore and sometimes set on fire, in the belief that the soul was released by the flame to fly even more quickly to the Viking equivalent of "paradise."

The fabulous Oseberg ship-grave yielded many wonderful pieces and may have been the grave of a Viking lady named Queen Asa. The Ynglinga Saga tells of a neighbor king named Gudrodr who asked Asa's father, Harald Redbeard, for his daughter in marriage. Harald's refusal caused King Gudrodr to sail back with an army of his men later, land undetected, and kill both Harald and his son,

Gyrr, at night in their home. Gudrodr then stole Asa and a large bounty, forcing her to marry him. A celebration cruise was taken and much drinking went on, both on board and on land. One night while docked in Stiflusund, the drunken king started to leave the boat but was killed by a spear. His men caught and killed the spear-wielder and by morning light identified the man as Queen Asa's servant. According to ancient Scandinavian customs, this was within Asa's rights. The family of the victims were allowed to avenge their deaths by right of the "blood oath."

During her life Queen Asa selected a bog on her farm as her burial site and this bog helped to preserve the wooden grave-goods, including the ship itself. A masterpiece of architecture and ornamentation, the ship was probably used as a luxury vessel staying close to shore rather than being

used as a sea-going vessel. On the prow of the boat are carvings of mysterious, curious animals. From each animal's round head protrudes a pigtail and from each open mouth comes a long tongue. Their bodies are shaped somewhat like a figure eight, and all are intertwined by the head or hindquarters of the animal above and below. Each figure's body is decorated with crisscross, checkered or parallel lines and the whole produces an intricate, rhythmic effect.

Remarkable carvings of birds and animals adorn sledges, a cart and ornamental wall hangings. Much has been written about the very skillful court artists' works. Four artists have been identified, indicating that the Vikings took their decorative art very seriously.

Another rich burial was found at Broa, again on the island of Gotland. Delightful animal designs decorate the mounts of bridles, a sword hilt and several other objects, all in bronze. Some of

these animals have lyre-shaped forms with double-contoured bodies, curved claws and openings through which long sprouts of "toes" and other tendrils appear. The "gripping beast" appears, too, in the Broa artifacts. This is a new motif and a very important one to early Scandinavian art. These are energetic animals that grip each other, themselves and the frames on all sides of them.

The next style, called Borre, uses the "gripping beast" more widely. This, too, was a burial site, but was a barrow grave. Spirits were believed to inhabit the barrow graves and the "gripping beasts" may represent guardians of the contents. Most of the pieces found in this Norwegian grave were in the form of metal brooches and fittings for horse trappings. The Borre style was popular during the same period as the Jellinge form. At times the two styles have been found on the same piece.

Ribbon-like bodies appear on the Jellinge animals; their heads are shown in profile with open mouths and a curlicue to the top lip. They sport long tongues and pigtails that weave through and become part of the pattern. The style was introduced into England by Scandinavian settlers and has been found on skillfully made jewelry and stone sculpture.

A much stockier animal, whose spiral hip joints have increased in size, is part of the Mammen period; a new lion-like figure, that has become known as the "great beast." Its body begins to accumulate more patterning in the form of dots, circles and pelleting. Long coils of snakes writhe in and around the body of what appears to be a lion or perhaps a wolf. Foliage crowns or tails appear and sometimes the sprouting simply twists and turns on its own in the background.

More prominent in the Ringerike period, foliage sometimes takes the shape of palmettes with pear-shaped lobes. The tendrils lengthen and cross each other in a more carefully orchestrated way. The "great beast" takes on a thinner, more stylized appearance and Ringerike is often found in combination with other styles, especially Urnes, the last true Viking art form.

A wonderfully ornamented eleventh-century church in western Norway was the name-place for the art known as Urnes. Considered to be the ultimate of early Scandinavian art, Urnes animals have become by this time very elegant and sleek. The forms begin to resemble greyhounds or deer, and dragons appear often. Seldom are there tendril clusters, but interlace now weaves regularly through the work in graceful, figure-eight designs. The animals have huge, pointed eyes, with upper and lower-lip lappets. The motif is one of combat, the animals warring with slim arrow-like snakes.

Carried to Britain and Ireland by early Scandinavian settlers, the Urnes and Ringerike styles both achieved great popularity. The Urnes design was so well liked by the Irish that they incorporated it for the first time into their own indigenous art. Manuscripts illuminated by Christian monks show signs of the Urnes period being integrated into their lettering.

Traditions, both pagan and Christian, were commonly being used together by the twelfth century. Churchmen found it much easier to effect lasting change by incorporating the old with the new. The ornamentation of the stave church portals is an example of this. These finely carved doorposts depict myth and legends both, along with luxurious vegetative forms and baroque animals and birds.

Stave churches take their name from the construction of vertical plank walls. Since this practice brought the wooden church walls in direct contact with the soil, only a few survive.

Some of those which remain have multiple roofs rather like the leaf canopies of Yggdrasil, the Scandinavian World Tree. The roofs' gables were set off by fierce animal and dragon heads meant to ward off evil spirits threatening the tender new Christian religion.

Another clue to the mingling of old and new is in the form of a widely used amulet known as "Thor's Hammer." Shaped like the mythical weapon used by the god of the peasants, some of these display the glaring eyes associated with the Thunder God, Thor. It is believed that the silver-hammer charms were used to seal a wedding vow; to consecrate a new home; or to celebrate the birth of a baby. As time went on, the hammer on a chain was reversed and became easily the motif of the new religion, that of the cross.

Gradually the new religion displaced the pagan beliefs altogether and the art was transformed into copies of the Christian art of the time. In other parts of the world, Viking art continued on for a time. Iceland, virtually uninhabited until the Vikings settled it beginning about 850-60 AD, was chosen to be a sanctuary for the Norse culture. Much of what we know today about these people and their art results from the fact that Iceland performed its sanctuary function so very well.

B.U.V.B.

Note: Since the styles overlap, it is not possible to give specific dates to each period. However, it is generally agreed that the dates given are quite close:

I	**Picture-stones**	*—fifth century on*
II	**Pre-Viking**	*— to 750*
III	**Broa**	*750-850*
IV	**Borre**	*830-960*
V	**Jellinge**	*875-975*
VI	**Mammen**	*950-1060*
VII	**Ringerike**	*975-1090*
VIII	**Urnes**	*1040-1150*
IX	**Late Viking**	*1150—*
X	**Stave Church**	*1000-1150*

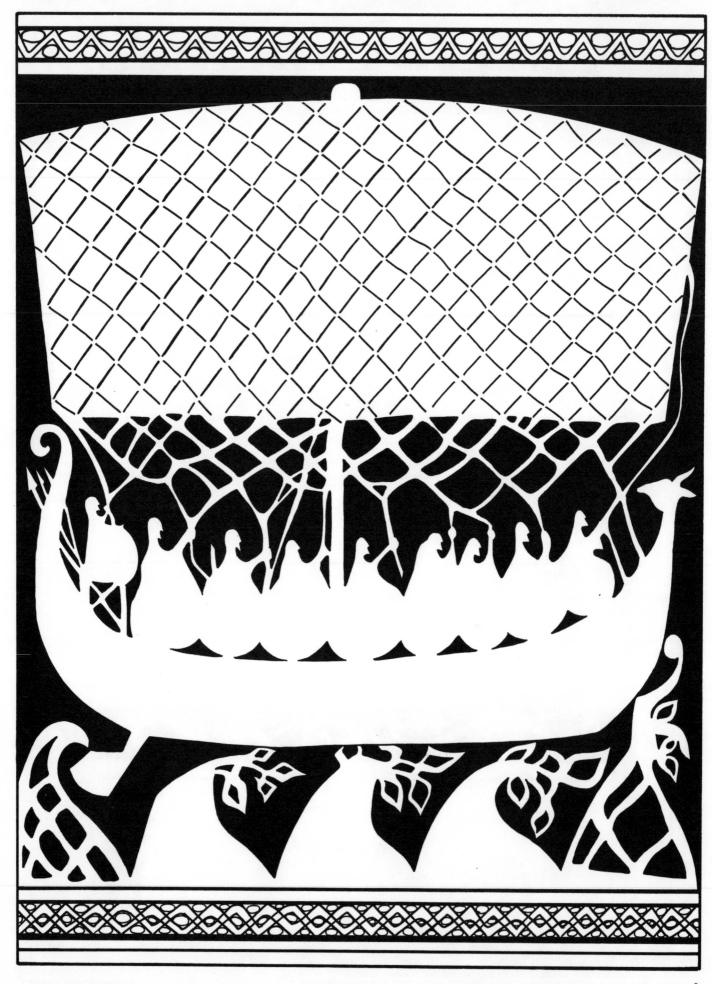

1

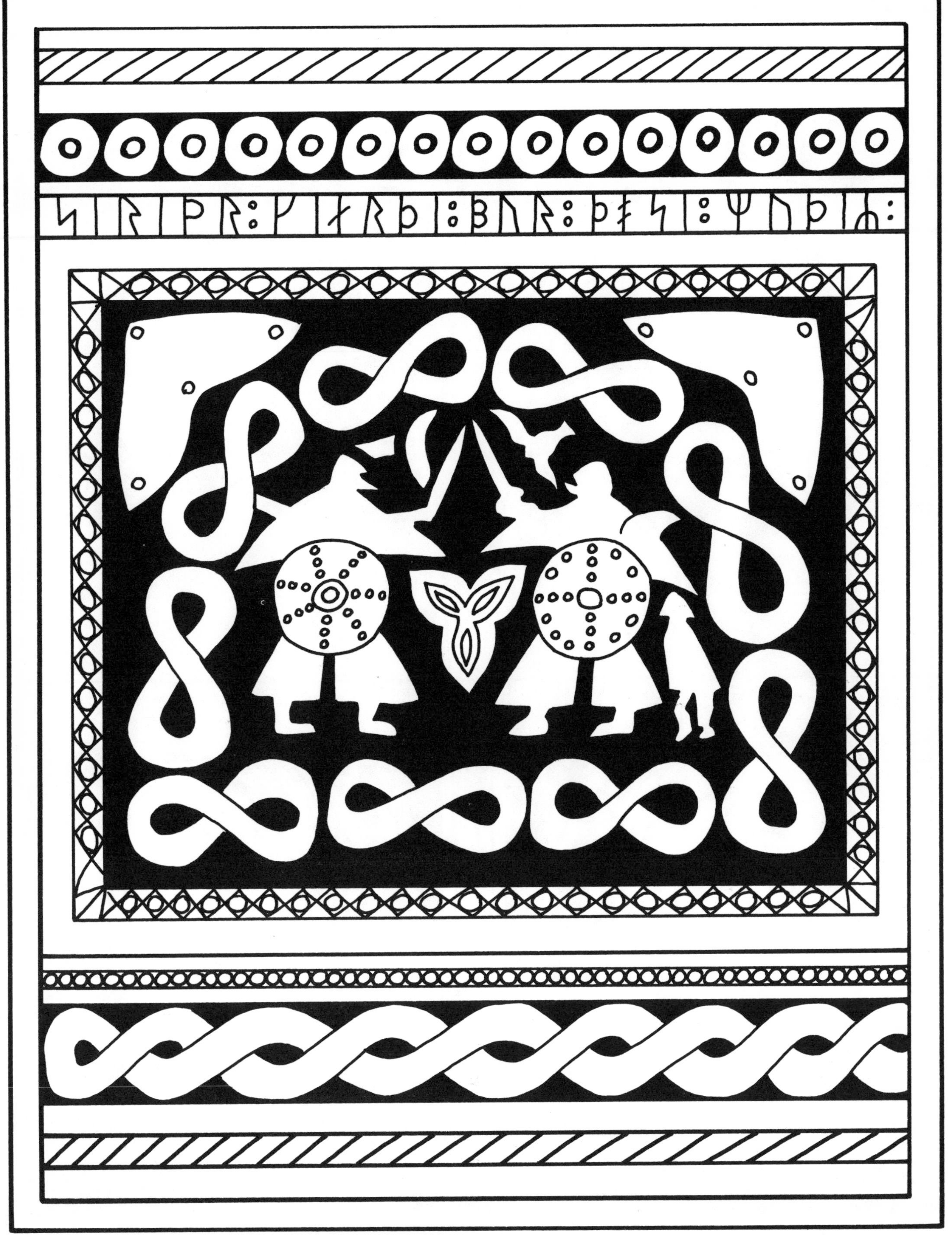

11

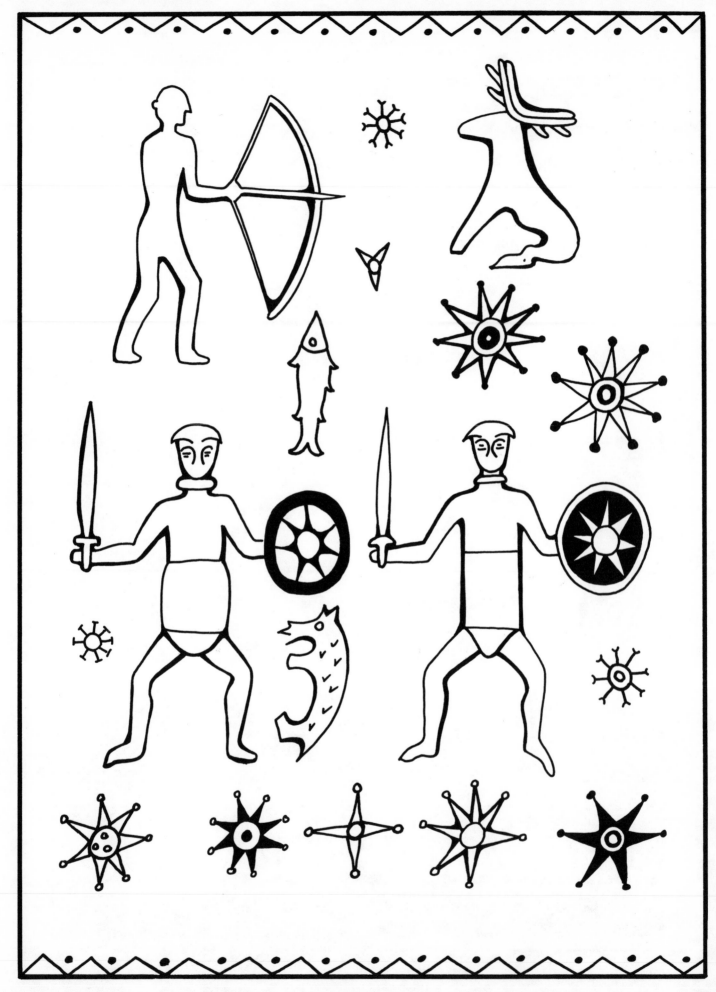

1

11

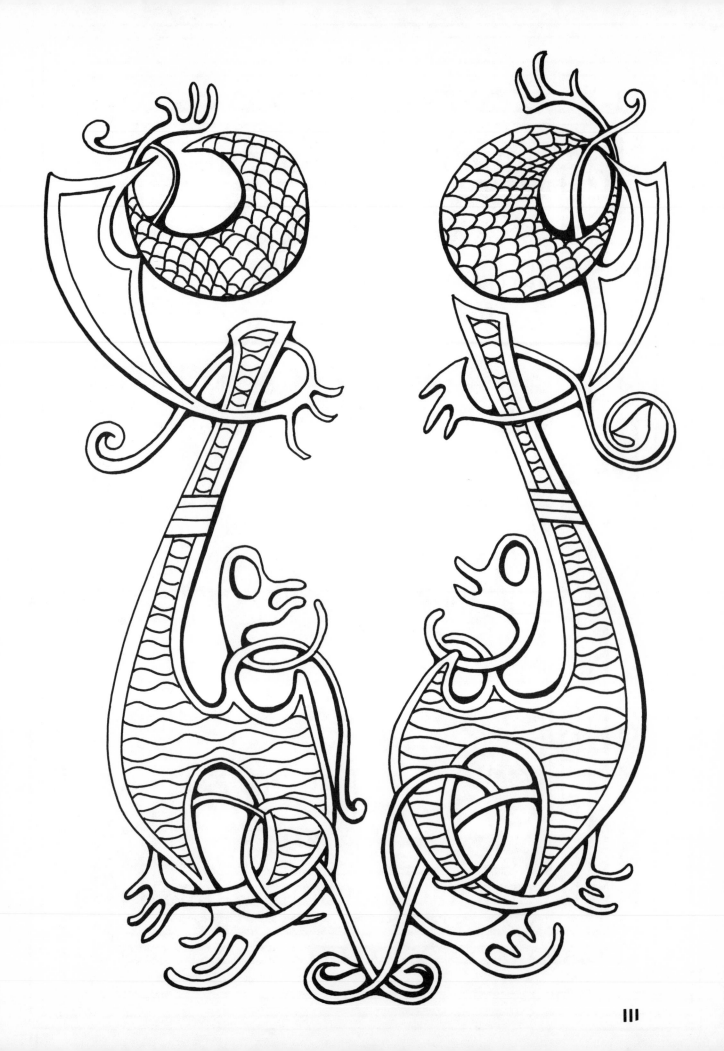

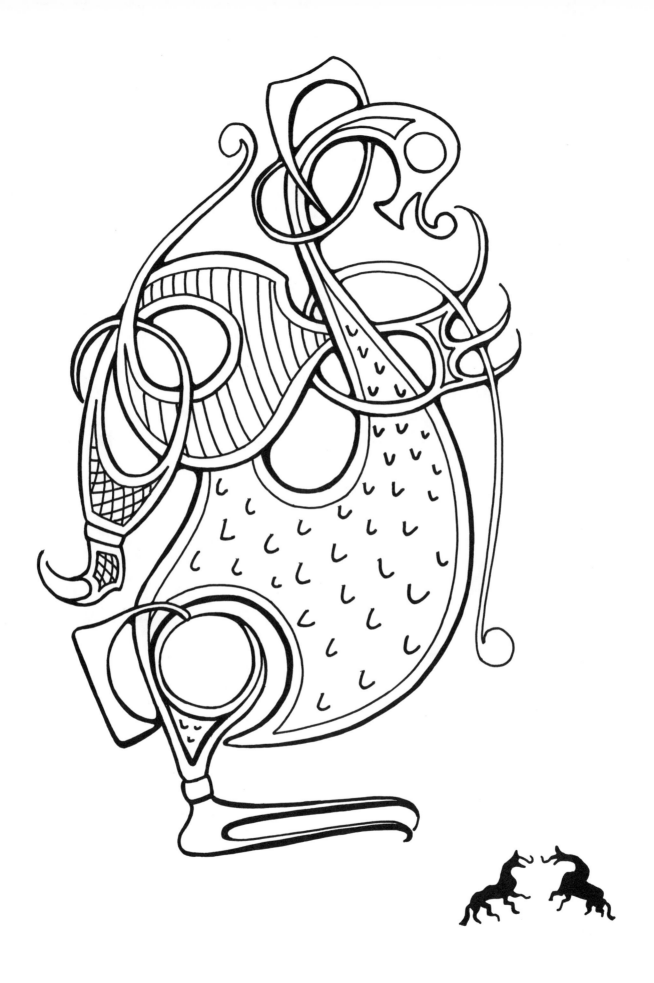

IV

IV

v

v

VI

VII

VIII

VIII

VIII

VIII

VIII

VIII

VIII

VIII

IX

X

X

IX

Designed by Barbara Holdridge
Composed in Times Roman by Brown Composition,
  Baltimore, Maryland
Printed on 75-pound Williamsburg Offset and
  bound by Victor Graphics, Inc., Baltimore, Maryland
Cover color separation by Sun Crown, Washington, D.C.
Cover printed by Strine Printing Company, York,
  Pennsylvania